Love

3 Books in 1

131
Creative Conversations
For Couples

131
Engaging Conversations
For Couples

131
Necessary Conversations
Before Marriage

www.CoffeeShopConversations.com

Creative, Christ-honoring
conversation starters to grow your
relationship and deepen your connection!

Also By Jed

131 Creative Conversations for Families

131 Conversations that Engage Kids

131 Boredom Busters and Creativity Builders

131 Stress Busters and Mood Boosters for Kids

Coffee Shop Conversations: Psychology and the Bible

Coffee Shop Inspirations: Simple Strategies for Building Dynamic Leadership and Relationships

131 Conversations for Stepfamily Success

Unlocking Stepfamily Success eCourse

Get Free Books

To thank you for your purchase, I would like to send you a free gift.

Transform from discouraged and burned out, to an enthusiastic agent of joy who parents at a higher–happier–level. _Be Happier Now_, provides ten, easy to apply, happiness strategies for reducing stress and increasing joy at home!

I will also make sure you are the first to know about free books and future deals!

www.coffeeshopconversations.com/happiness/

Contents

♥ ♥ ♥

131 Creative Conversations
For Couples

131 Engaging Conversations
For Couples

131 Necessary Conversation
Before Marriage

♥ ♥ ♥

131
Creative Conversations
For Couples

Christ-honoring questions to
deepen your relationship,
grow your friendship,
and kindle romance.

Jed Jurchenko

www.CoffeeShopConversations.com

Introduction
The Power of Connection

Love, friendship, and romance are fundamental ingredients to a lasting relationship. While they are by no means the only factors, they are essential. A relationship lacking these qualities is like baking brownies and leaving out the chocolate, eggs, or sugar. When key components are missing, a decadent treat becomes dull and bland.

Sadly, "dull and bland," sum up far too many relationships. I remember the dean of our seminary proclaiming, "The loneliest people in America are not the single adults. They are married couples, who fall asleep–back-to-back, thinking to themselves, *when is this emptiness going to end?*'" His words are packed with truth. Single adults have the hope of meeting that special someone and living happily ever after.

Feeling trapped in a tasteless, pancakes with no syrup, toast without the butter, hospital-mush relationship is depressing. The good news is that if your relationship is in a slump, it doesn't have to stay that way. Moreover, if you are one of those fortunate couples who already have a loving connection to their best friend, the questions in this book will assist you in building upon your solid foundation.

Mixing in the Key Ingredients

Love, friendship, and romance--three key ingredients of a happy relationship–share the common thread of intimacy. My favorite definition of intimacy is, "in-to-me-see." It is the ability to peer into the heart of another, while simultaneously allowing that person to gaze into your inner world.

In an intimate relationship, two people know each other inside and out, or to use a Biblical phrase, "the two become one." The intimate couple chooses to accept each other as is, warts and all. They make the intentional decision to find joy as a couple. This level of intimacy builds over time. It is the result of a mutual sharing of:

- Feelings
- Dreams

- Desires
- Fears
- Future aspirations
- Hopes, and
- Casual thoughts

Intimacy happens at the intersection of the casual, deep, and spiritual. From the simple knowledge of the other person's favorite meal to understanding their deep fears and connection to their creator, intimacy covers everything.

Yet, knowledge alone is not enough. Knowing is only the first step to a joyful partnership. When I envision an intimate relationship, I imagine:

- A couple in their nineties, strolling hand-in-hand along the seashore.
- A young couple–juggling multiple jobs and a house full of kids–who long to spend every spare moment in each other's presence.
- An established couple in their fifties– settled into the routine of life–who considers their time together to be the highlight of their week.

Love is an action word. The purpose of gaining deeper knowledge is to improve our acts of love. It is our daily demonstrations of love--shown through a playful, joyful, friendship--that matter most. This is where intimacy leads. The destination is two people who know one another fully, care for each other deeply, and are excited about spending time in each other's presence.

Fostering Intimacy

The questions in this book are designed to foster intimacy. In the pages ahead, you will find 131 open-ended questions. This means that more than a simple "yes" or "no" answer will be required. Many questions are followed up with the question "why?" in order to mine deeper into your partner's heart.

Working through this book as a couple is a gift. It is the gift of time, the gift of knowledge, and most of all, the gift of you. Back when my wife and I began dating, I kept a similar book of questions in my car. Jenny and I worked through each inquiry-- one by one--over a number of weeks. We shared our hopes, dreams, and outlook on life. We laughed in coffee shops, chatted on dinner dates, and took turns asking questions while relaxing at the beach.

These times of mutual sharing were a highlight of our two-and-a-half years of dating. Now that we are married, Jenny and I continue to ask excellent questions. Of course, this is expected when a social worker and therapist unite.

As I researched other books on questions for couples, I noticed three primary complaints. Some books include R-rated material that was embarrassing and stirred up conflict. Others contained questions quickly answered with a simple "yes" or "no." The result was an experience that felt more like an interrogation than an intimate connection. Finally, older couples reported that, in many cases, they already knew what their partner's reply would be. As a result, these couples breezed through the book without deep discussion taking place.

This book is different. Every question will stir up conversations that extend beyond what you already know. As a marriage and family therapist and seminary professor, I am good at asking questions. I packed this book with creative, share your inner-world, type of questions. Whether you are in the beginning stages of your relationship or approaching your golden anniversary, this book will lead you to deeper levels of intimacy and add value to your lives.

Getting Started

In the pages ahead, you will find 131 questions for deepening your love, friendship, and romance. There are no rules attached. My suggestion is that the two of you work through these questions one at a time, over a number of dates.

Date ideas include:

- Picnics in the park
- Outings to a favorite restaurant. (Try going through a question or two while waiting for your meal).
- Bring this book with you on road-trips.

- Keep a copy in your purse or on your smart-phone. Pull it out whenever there is a lull in the conversation.
- Keep a copy on your kitchen table and dive into a question over breakfast each morning.
- Ask these questions during an evening bonfire.
- Walk to a coffee shop together and work through the book while enjoying a favorite beverage.
- Arrive at a movie early and go through a few questions while you wait for the show to start.

As you work through this book, here are some connection strategies to keep in mind.

Take your time. There is nothing magical about these questions and no prize for finishing the book. The reward is in the bonding. So, by all means, slow down and enjoy the process. If the two of you find yourselves engaged in conversation, set the book down, and keep talking—you are doing things right.

Turn toward your partner. This is also known as having good micro-skills. Micro-skills are the nonverbal ways that we communicate, "I am interested in you." Experts estimate that anywhere from fifty to ninety percent of our communication takes place nonverbally. Thus, you will want to pay careful attention to this area. Here is a quick breakdown of essential micro-skills that will amplify your connection:

- Sit with an open posture, with arms and legs uncrossed.
- Turn your body toward your partner.
- Make steady eye contact.
- Smile.
- Ask open-ended questions that encourage discussion.
- Turn your cell-phone off, and give your partner the gift of distraction-free time.

Strive for understanding. This book is not about working through long-standing issues nor getting caught-up in heated disagreements. Instead, it is meant to foster an appreciation for similarities, differences, and to create a greater understanding of each person's unique contribution to the relationship. Opposites attract. If you and your partner shared similar thinking in all areas, one of you wouldn't be needed. Everybody has the need to feel heard and understood. Practice validating your partner's feeling and watch your intimacy grow.

Have fun! William Glasser, the renowned therapist and founder of choice theory, listed "fun" as one of the five basic human needs. Fun is serious business. Remember, you are connecting with someone that you care about deeply. So, enjoy these moments to the fullest!

Some of the questions in this book are serious. Others lighten the mood. All of them facilitate connection.

Ecclesiastes 4:9-10 says, "Two people are better than one, because they can reap more benefit from their labor. For if they fall, one will help his companion up, but pity the person who falls down and has no one to help him up."

A couple that teams-up to strengthen their love, friendship, and romance, is pursuing a worthy goal. My prayer is that as you dive into these questions, the two of you develop a deeper bond than ever before!

Sincerely,

COFFEE SHOP CONVERSATIONS

131
Creative Conversations For Couples

Ask the right questions if you're going to find the right answers.

~ Vanessa Redgrave

Counsel in a person's heart is like deep water, but an understanding person draws it out.

~ Proverbs 20:5

Question #1

Imagine that you could send a letter back in time to your younger self. What would your message say and to which year would you send it?

Question #2

Growing up, what was one of your favorite family traditions? Describe what made this time extra special.

Question#3

Imagine that on your next birthday, your rich uncle tells you that his present to you is the gift of a perfect day. Then, he hands you his credit card. For the next 24 hours, there are no limits to what you can spend. Where will you go, what will you do, and whom will you take with you?

Question #4

If you had to choose between the two, would you rather die exactly three years from today or live so long that you outlast all of your friends? Why?

Question #5

Describe the most adventurous thing you have ever done. If you were given the opportunity, would you do this again?

Question #6

Describe an adventurous activity that you would like to do in the future. What makes this particular adventure so appealing?

Question #7

Who was your childhood best friend and what was it that made this relationship so special?

Question #8

Most teenagers have the occasional awkward moments. Describe an embarrassing moment from your teenage years.

Question #9

Growing up, what household rule did you dislike the most and why?

Question #10

Growing up, what household rule benefited you the most? Why was this rule helpful, and will you pass it on to your own children?

Question #11

Describe a childhood mentor, teacher, or coach who had a positive impact on your life. What was it that this person said or did that was so meaningful?

Question #12

Imagine a genie from a magic lamp grants you one life do-over. What past event would you change, and how would you do things differently?

Question #13

If you could have dinner with a present-day hero, who would you dine with and why?

Love is patient, Love is Kind...
~1 Corinthians 13:4

Question #14

If you could travel back in time and dine with any historical figure, who would you eat with and why?

Question #15

In your opinion, what is one mistake that your parents made in raising you? How will you do things differently with your own children?

Question #16

What is one thing that your parents did right in raising you? Why was this so meaningful?

Question #17

Describe a time in your life when you felt especially close to God. Why do you think you felt so close to God during this particular season of life?

You know you're in love when you can't fall asleep because reality is finally better than your dreams.
~Dr. Seuss

Question #18

What are you currently doing to nurture yourself spiritually? Are there spiritual activities that you did in the past that you miss?

Question #19

If you had to decide between a career filled with money and fame--where you are away from your family 200+ days a year--or a career where you are relatively unknown, but are able to return to your family at the end of the day, which one would you choose and why?

Question #20

If you could visit anywhere in the world, where would it be and why?

Question #21

Growing up, what were some of your favorite childhood toys and television shows?

Question #22

Describe one accomplishment that you are especially proud of?

Question #23

Imagine that you have the ability to peer into the future. Describe what your life looks like exactly five years from today. What career are you working? Who are your friends? What are your hobbies, and how are you spending the majority of your time?

Question #24

Now, imagine that you peer even further into the future. Describe what your life looks like ten years from today.

Question #25

Would you rather be unable to have children at all, or only be able to birth quadruplets? Why?

Question #26

Who is one couple that you admire, and what makes this couple's relationship great?

Question #27

Describe what it was like for you when your parents were angry with each other?

Question #28

Growing up, what was it like when your parents were angry with you? What will you do differently when you become angry with your own children?

Question #29

What do you do when you get angry with someone you care about? Is this similar or different than your parent's style of anger? Why?

Question #30

Describe a perfect date night. What would you do? Where would you go? Whom would you take with you?

Question #31

When you are in a bad mood, what is one simple thing your partner can do to brighten your day?

Question #32

Who is your best friend right now? What is it that you like most about this friend?

Question #33

What is one book that influenced your life? How did this book help shape you and your worldview?

Question #34

Imagine that you are mentoring a troubled teen and have the opportunity to offer one piece of advice. What wisdom would you share?

Question #35

If you were asked to offer one piece of spiritual advice in church, what recommendation would you give? What makes this advice important to you personally?

Question #36

In your opinion, why do so many marriages fail?

Question #37

In America, the divorce rate is nearly 50 percent. What do you believe it takes to make a marriage last?

Question #38

What do you consider the most important qualities of a lasting friendship? How are you at demonstrating these qualities yourself?

Question #39

What political party do you most closely associate with and why?

Question #40

What spiritual beliefs are most important to you and why?

Question #41

Imagine that you will be stranded on a deserted island for a year. You are allowed to take one personal item with you. What would you bring and why?

Question #42

What is one food that you would happily eat every day for the next year?

Question #43

What are some of life's simple pleasures that make you smile?

Question #44

What is one wrong in the world that you are passionate about changing for the better?

Question #45

If you could have one superhuman power, what would it be? How would you use it?

Question #46

Imagine that you are appointed president of the United States for one hour and have the ability to enact one law. What law would you make or change? Why?

Question #47

What Bible story or passage of Scripture is especially meaningful to you and why?

Question #48

What is one decision that you regret making, and what do you wish you had done differently?

Question #49

If you were to create a bucket list, what would your top 3-5 items be?

Question #50

Imagine that a rich uncle passes away. His last wish was to donate his multi-million dollar fortune to charity. However, no charity was designated in the will and you are asked to distribute his wealth. What charities will you donate to and why?

♥ ♥ ♥
Love is like the wind,
you can't see it but you can feel it
~Nicholas Sparks

Question #51

What hobby or activity do you believe will play an important part in your life as long as you live? Why is this activity so important to you?

Question #52

If you won $1000 today, would you be more likely to take a vacation, make a purchase, pay down bills, or save it? Why?

Question 53

Do you believe there is such a thing as "good debt?" If so, what things are worth going into debt over?

Question #54

Who is that happiest person you know? What do you think makes this person so upbeat?

Question #55

If you created a list of the things you are most afraid of, what would be the top 3 items on this list?

Question #56

Do you consider yourself a happy person? If so, what do you do to stay in a good mood? If not, what would it take to make you happy?

Question #57

If you had to choose to go through the remainder of your life with either no arms or no legs, which would you choose and why?

Question #58

When you were a child, how did you answer the question, "What do you want to be when you grow up?" Has your answer changed over time?

Question #59

If you could have any job in the world, what would it be, and why?

Question #60

When was the last time you felt embarrassed? Describe what happened that made you feel this way.

Question #61

When is the last time you felt happy? What made you feel this way?

Question #62

Are there any causes or people that you feel so passionate about that you would be willing to die for them? If so, what or who are they?

Question #63

Imagine you find yourself standing before God and He asks, "Why should I let you into heaven?" What would you say?

Question #64

If you could ask God any one question, what would it be? Why?

Question #65

How were you disciplined as a child? Will (or do) you discipline your own children in a similar manner? Why or why not?

Question #66

Imagine that you have a thriving career as a therapist. Every day you meet with clients who are drug addicts, domestic-violence victims, mentally ill, and in the prison system. Are there any types of client's that you would absolutely refuse to meet with? If so, who would you be unwilling to meet with and why?

Question #67

In your opinion, what is the best way to instill positive values in children?

Question #68

If you could be remembered for only one thing, what would you like to be known for?

Question #69

When you find yourself sad, mad, or frustrated, is it easy or difficult to share how you are feeling with others? Why do you think talking about how you feel does or does not come naturally for you?

Question #70

Describe a time in your life when you were afraid? If you were afraid right now, how would those around you know?

Question #71

Would you rather go through life not being able to see or not being able to hear, and why?

Question #72

Which holiday is your favorite, and what is one of your most cherished holiday memories?

Question #73

Imagine that your significant other says they want to make this Valentine's Day the best ever. What would he or she do to make the day extra special?

Question #74

If you were asked to give helpful advice to a couple who is arguing continually, what would you say to them?

Question #75

How do you know if someone is trustworthy? Do you consider yourself a trustworthy person?

Question #76

Describe a favorite childhood vacation. What was it that made this getaway so special?

Question #77

If you were going through a difficult time and needed to seek out wise advice, who would you turn to, and why?

Question #78

What are you currently doing to make this world a better place? If you can't think of anything, what types of things would you like to do in the future?

To love is to be vulnerable.
~ C.S.Lewis

Question #79

Imagine that you have the opportunity to listen to your own eulogy. What types of statements do you hope are being made about you?

Question #80

Who is one person that you would like to model your life after? What are the specific qualities this person has that you would like to build into your own life?

Question #81

What do you consider to be your greatest strengths?

Question #82

What do you consider to be your greatest weaknesses?

Question #83

If you had the opportunity to give our current president one piece of advice, what suggestion would you give?

Question #84

Most everyone has at least a few "hot buttons," or little things that easily annoy them. What are some of yours?

Question #85

Do you believe that men and women should hold traditional gender roles today? (Such as the man being the primary "bread-winner" for the family and the woman being a homemaker and primary caregiver for the children). Why, or why not?

Question #86

Growing up, did your parents follow traditional gender roles? Do you believe this had a positive or negative impact on their overall relationship?

Question #87

Every family has their own unique family culture. Describe some of the important aspects of your family's culture growing up.

"Where there is love there is life."
~ Mahatma Gandhi

Question #88

Describe the type of family culture that you would ideally like to have.

Question #89

"Children should be seen and not heard." Do you agree with this statement? Why, or why not?

Question #90

What types of things make a movie or television show offensive to you? Have you ever gone to a movie that was so offensive that you decided to walk out?

Question #91

In your opinion, what type of activities do a spiritually healthy couple participate in together? Are there any spiritual activities that you would like to start doing together as a couple?

♥ ♥ ♥
Love does no wrong to a neighbor.
~ Romans 13:10

Question #92

Have you ever been the victim of discrimination, bullying, or racism? If so, what happened, and how did it make you feel?

Question #93

If you had to choose a career other than the one you are currently in, what job would you choose, and why?

Question #94

Imagine that you receive a call from the local zoo stating that they are closing down. All of their animals--including the exotic ones--are up for adoption. Which animal or animals would you adopt, and how would you care for them?

Question #95

If your loved one wanted to do something simple to show you he or she cared, what would this look like?

Question #96

What is one religious belief that your church holds that you disagree with?

Question #97

If you had to choose between the two, would you rather have:

A. A few close friends whom you know well.

B. Many friends with whom you have a surface level relationships.

Why?

Question #98

If you and your partner were getting over a big fight, what is one small step that your partner could take to begin making amends?

Question #99

What one movie do you think everyone should see, and why?

Question #100

On a scale of 1-10, with 1 being not very important and 10 being extremely important, how essential is your faith to you?

Question #101

How old were you when you started driving? Do you believe that this is a good age for kids to learn to drive today? Why, or why not?

Question #102

If you were to pick a fictional television family that you would most like your own family to resemble, which family would it be, and why?

Question #103

Describe the worst date you ever had. What it was that made this particular date so bad?

Question #104

From your perspective, what does it mean for a couple to fight fair?

Question #105

In your opinion, what does it look like when a couple fights dirty?

Question #106

How would you describe your own conflict style? Is it fair, dirty, or a mixture of both?

Question #107

What is one conflict that you've had that you feel was resolved well? What is it that made the conflict resolution work?

Question #108

If you could change any one thing about your physical appearance, what would it be, and why?

Question #109

In your opinion, what is one area of our relationship that we could work on together to make our connection even stronger?

Question #110

If you knew you were going to die at this exact time tomorrow, how would you spend the next 24 hours?

Question #111

Do you believe in love at first sight? Why, or why not?

Question #112

What do you think are the most important things parents can do to raise great kids?

Question #113

What do you like best about our current relationship?

Question #114

If you learned that one week from today you would suddenly lose your ability to see, how would you spend the next week?

Question #115

If you had to choose between a career you love that pays just over minimum wage or a job you despise that will make you rich, which would you choose, and why?

Question #116

Growing up, what were some of your favorite childhood stories and books?

Question #117

Imagine that you woke up one morning and discovered that you had traveled back in time to the day after you graduated from high school. As you move forward and relive your life, what is one thing that you would do differently? What is one thing that you would do exactly the same?

Question #118

In your opinion, what is the single most important ingredient to making a relationship work?

Question #119

How old were you when you got your first cell phone? At what age do you think it is appropriate for children to have their own phone?

Question #120

What is one life experience you had that was so amazing, you would relive it if you could?

Question #121

What has been one challenging experience in your life that has resulted in you becoming a better person? In what ways did this incident help you improve yourself?

Question #122

What is one of your favorite childhood memories with one or both of your parents? What makes this particular memory so meaningful to you?

Question #123

In most families, members take on a family role. There is the black-sheep, who is always blamed for the problems, the hero, who can do no wrong, the judge, who mediates to keep the peace, and the nurse, who comforts those who are hurting. What image would you use to describe your role in your family as you grew up?

Question #124

How would you describe your role in your family now that you are an adult? Do you think your role has changed?

Question #125

What was your parent's attitude toward alcohol growing up? In what ways is your attitude toward alcohol the same as or different than that of your parents?

Question #126

Would you describe your life as easy, average, or exceptionally difficult? Why?

Question #127

What single activity brings you the most joy in life?

Question #128

What life circumstances currently cause you the most pain?

Question #129

If you were to take a small step to improve your circumstances in this painful area, what would that look like?

Question #130

If you had to choose between getting in a big, blow-up argument that resolved the problem quickly or quietly resolving the problem over a matter of days, which would you choose, and why?

Question #131

What did you like best about going through the questions in this book with your significant other?

Keeping Love Going

I hope these relationships questions have been enjoyable and that you have gained new insights into the inner world of the person you care about deeply. If so, congratulations! The goal of this book was to stir up conversations leading to deeper levels of connection, and you have succeeded!

But, don't stop here. Intimacy is an ongoing journey. Stay curious about your loved one, and remember to keep sharing your inner world as well. You can find additional resources for growing your love on our website:

www.coffeeshopconversations.com

131
Engaging Conversations
For Couples

Christ-honoring conversation starters to
strengthen your family bond.

Jed Jurchenko

www.CoffeeShopConversations.com

Connection Secrets of Happy Couples

Envision waking up next to the person you care about most in the world. Imagine how it would feel to traverse through life, hand-in-hand, with your best friend. This person is aware of your successes, failures, hopes, dreams, and fears. Yet, in spite of all of these things, and because of these things, he or she loves you deeply. In short, the two of you are profoundly connected.

Naturally, this type of bond does not mean the two of you see eye-to-eye on everything. Yet, you find this perfectly acceptable. Opposites attract, and if you both always had the same outlook, then one of you would not be necessary. For this reason, in your relationship, differences are celebrated.

One of the best parts of your connection is its steadiness. Yours is not a relational rollercoaster, where moments of closeness are interrupted by fiery rage or icy coldness.

Instead, you are reliable confidants who are always on each other's side.

Of course, your relationship is not seven days a week of nonstop bliss—that would be exhausting. Instead, it is more like a cozy sweater that you can always count on for comfort and warmth. There is a peace that comes from knowing you could make a dumb mistake—even an extraordinarily dumb mistake—and your partner would welcome you with open arms, stating, "Honey, I am so sorry this happened."

Five years from now, the two of you will continue to be madly in love. You believe this with all of your heart. Fifty your from now, you picture yourselves still strolling, hand-in-hand through the park. For some, a truly happy relationship sounds too good to be true. Fortunately, this type of close connection is not reserved for fairytales. It is available to every couple willing to learn to connect in three significant ways.

The Secret of Happy Relationships

Happy, secure relationships do not

happen by accident. These couples have a secret to their success. They know how to connect well. This is accomplished by connecting often, connecting intimately, and reconnecting quickly whenever a disruption occurs. These three connection principles are the foundation of nearly every happy relationship.

The goal of this book is to support you and your partner in connecting in each of these vital ways. I use the term partner because this book is for all couples. I am a firm believer that it is never too early, nor too late to strengthen your bond. Whether you are on your first date, approaching your golden anniversary, or somewhere in between, these conversation starters are designed to assist you in drawing closer together than ever before.

Like exercising in order to build muscle mass, the connection to our loved one grows with intentional effort. On the other hand, if you and I lounge in front of the television, gorge on potato chips, and act as though our partner does not exist, then our connection will slowly wither away. This book is for couples who are willing to take action by exercising their connection muscles. Before diving into the conversations, let's first examine what connection is, and why each of the three connection components is vital.

Connection Defined

I define connection as any activity that causes you and your partner to draw closer together. If feelings of love, warmth, and friendship increase, then a connecting moment has occurred. To understand the value of connectedness, it may help to visualize a love-bank built into your partner's heart. Love-bank deposits are made every time your partner feels cared for. On the other hand, when he or she feels disrespected, taken for granted, hurt, or unloved, then a love-bank withdrawal occurs.

It is important to note that love-bank deposits and withdrawals center around your partner's feelings. They are not based on your intentions. If your loved one feels disrespected, then you have made a withdrawal, even if your motives were pure.

Positive and negative transactions are a normal part of all relationships. Similar to traditional banking, love-bank goals should include making regular deposits, building a healthy savings, and never allowing one's balance to fall into the negative. In love-banking terms, a zero-balance means that your partner no longer feels valued by you, and this is a perilous state for any relationship.

It is important to note that the love-bank is not a method of keeping score. Nor is it a tit-for-tat mentality that says, "I did something nice for you, so later, you must return the favor." Instead, the love-bank metaphor is a vivid reminder that the people we care about will not feel valued if we do not act in loving ways toward them. Remember, love is an action word.

The skills of connecting often, connecting intimately, and reconnecting quickly are strategies that happy couples employ to fill each other's love-banks. Now, let's explore why each of these three areas is vital to a healthy, vibrant relationship.

Happy Couples Connect Often

A common relationship myth is that high-quality interactions make up for a lack of significant time together. It is the age-old debate of whether quality time or quantity time together is most important. The bottom line is that both are necessary, and the two cannot be separated. Powerful connection moments happen when we least expect them, which is why connecting often is essential.

Years ago, before Jenny and I married, the two of us went hiking down a long stretch of deserted beach. Five miles into our trek, we paused for a picnic lunch. Afterward, we headed back to our car. Up to this point, the trip was pleasant. However, it was at the tail end of our journey that the big magic happened.

Suddenly, a pod of dolphin came bounding through the waves, less than fifty feet from shore. Jenny and I were ecstatic and paused to take in the moment. We assumed the dolphins would pass by quickly, but they didn't. Apparently, they were as enthralled by us as we were by them. When we resumed our stroll, the dolphins followed along, keeping perfect time. They entertained themselves by jumping over waves and enchanted us with their chatter. Finally, after a good deal of time had passed, the dolphins swam off toward the setting sun.

Magical moments like this simply cannot be planned. Our hike down the beach turned into an extraordinarily joyful memory and a powerful moment of connection that Jenny and I will forever cherish. I share this simple story because it illustrates why connecting often is necessary.

Designed to Connect

You and I are God-designed to connect. The book of Genesis describes how, after creating the heavens and the earth, God brought every animal before Adam, in what appears to be the very first relational experiment. Adam named each pair of beasts and noted that none was fit to be his lifelong companion. Then, God stated, "It is not good for the man to be alone. I will make a companion for him who corresponds to him."[1] God caused Adam to fall into a deep sleep before fashioning Eve, the first woman, out of Adam's own rib. The bottom line is that you and I are hardwired by God to connect.

Strategies for Connecting Often

Some couples connect by carving out large chunks of time together all at once. Others orchestrate small, frequent interactions throughout the day. The important thing is to keep the positive exchanges flowing. Connecting builds trust. It is also when hilarious inside jokes form, and where deep conversations flow naturally.

In connecting often, remember that feelings follow actions. On days you are tired, frustrated, or simply do not feel like putting forth the effort, try laying your protests aside and connecting anyway. Likely, it will not be long before the two of you are having a blast!

As you move through this book, you will notice that some conversation starters are purely for fun. There is an important reason for this. Not every conversation needs to have a purpose. If the two of you are connecting, solely for the joy of connecting, then you are doing things right. Be a couple that makes connecting the norm, because this is how lasting love forms.

Happy Couples Connect Intimately

Although society sometimes associates the word intimacy with sex, this is not how it is used in this book. None of the conversations are intended to make you blush. Instead, intimacy is defined as in-to-me-see. It is the ability to know our partner deeply while simultaneously allowing ourselves to be known.

Intimacy forms through a mutual sharing of hopes, dreams, fears, and failures. Being fully known, and fully loved is powerful. It allows us to run toward our partner instead of away from him or her during times of distress.

For me, intimacy is a game changer. As a busy daddy of four girls, I get scatterbrained often, and goofs are far more common than I would like to admit. Not long ago, I shuttled our two older girls from their slumber parties, to soccer games, and ice-skating lessons. Along the way, the girls and I stopped at home for lunch. Before rushing inside, I gathered an armful of garbage from the van–the kind of trash that endlessly appears out of nowhere when kids are around. Unfortunately, in my haste to clean, I inadvertently dropped our keys into the garbage bin.

It was not until after lunch that I realized that the keys were missing. This resulted in an all-out family search. Fortunately, after much hunting, the missing keys were found and the girls made it to their next event, albeit slightly late. The bright side of this whole debacle is that I was able to freely own up to my mistake. Never did I feel like I needed to try to cover up my blunder. Later that evening, Jenny and I laughed about the incident.

Jenny reminded me that, in the scheme of things, momentarily losing our keys in the garbage is not that bad. She recalled how she left a previous set of keys on our van roof. As our family cruised down the highway, a compassionate driver pulled alongside us. In one hand, he held up a single key that he had removed from his keychain, as he feverishly pointed to the roof. Although we took the next exit, it was too late. Our keys were long gone.

In our home, goofs are common. Fortunately, so is grace. Intimacy is all about grace. It says, "I know you. I see who you are, and I love you—mistakes and all."

God-Designed for Intimacy

Romans 5:8 says, "But God demonstrates his own love for us, in that while we were still sinners, Christ died for us." You and I are fully known, fully accepted, and fully loved by God. This is intimacy at its best.

Intimate relationships are the safest place to be. Some of the conversation starters in this book are designed to stir up intimacy by helping you peer into your partner's hopes, dreams, fears, and failures. As you move through the questions, lay aside the desire to change your partner, and to fix longstanding issues. Instead, get curious. Listen with empathy. Ask good follow-up questions, and whenever possible, accept your partner for whom he or she is. Doing this is precisely what will take your relationship to a deeper level.

Happy Couples Reconnect Quickly

According to marriage researcher John Gottman, happy couples excel at repair attempts.[2] Repair attempts are what allow couples to reconnect quickly after a relational disruption. One might say that happy couples know how to connect like Velcro.

If you take a close look at this unique fabric, you will notice that one side contains many minute hooks, while the other side has an abundance of tiny loops on which these hooks fasten. As a child, I remember being fascinated by Velcro. I would see how close I could place the strips to each other before they would begin to connect. Apparently, some of the hooks and loops stretch out further than the others do, because the entire system joins almost magically. It is as if the hooks and loops reach out for each other.

This is exactly how happy couples connect and reconnect–they reach for each other. This might happen through a shared joke, gentle touch, kind gesture, or a soft smile. The specific technique a couple uses to reconnect is unimportant. What matters is that each person actively seeks to reestablish the bond. Unhappy couples take the opposite approach. They return unkind gesture for unkind gesture, spiraling into an escalating pattern of love-bank withdrawals.

Happy and Unhappy Couples in Action

Now, let's take a look at happy couples and unhappy couples in action. A common, unhappy interaction will look like this: She makes a negative statement. He reacts by rolling his eyes. She counters with a critical remark. He feels overwhelmed and shuts down. This pattern continues for hours, days, weeks, or even years. Both partners push each other away, and each is miserable.

Happy couples implement simple repair attempts that disrupt this pattern. Let's look at one way a happy couple might utilize a repair attempt to reconnect. The scenario begins the same: She makes a negative comment. He rolls his eyes. She begins to counter with a critical comment but catches herself. Instead, she rolls her eyes back, while sticking out her tongue, and making a silly face—this is the repair attempt. He smiles back and makes an even more ridiculous face in return—thus receiving and reciprocating the repair attempt. At this point, the couple bursts into outrageous laughter. They have reached an unspoken agreement to cease the love-bank withdraws and to reunite.

Diving Deeper into Reconnection

In regards to the previous scenario, a quick word of caution is necessary. Eye rolling and silly faces will not work for every couple. Some people would view these gestures as additional insults. Thus, it is necessary to find repair attempts that fit the personality of you and your partner. In this case, the man knows that rolling his eyes is rude. When the woman rolls her eyes and makes a silly face in return, she is communicating, "I see you trying to be hurtful, but instead of making an issue about this, I am going to let go of my hurt and make a joke." He reciprocates, nonverbally communicating, "I like your humor, and I am willing to let go of my hurt too."

Reconnecting and Scripture

In Ephesians 4:26, the Bible affirms the value of being quick to forgive. This passage states, "Be angry and do not sin; do not let the sun go down on the cause of your anger." As you will see, some of the questions in this book hone-in on reconnecting during the stressful moments of life. While happy couples are not connected all of the time, they are connected most of the time. They excel at repair attempts, connecting like Velcro, by reaching out to each other after relational disruptions occur.

Christ, the Connection Foundation

You may have noticed that each of these connection principles is grounded in Scripture. This is because God knows how we function best. Thus, making Christ the center of your relationship is vital. He is the foundation on which each connection principles rests.

Colossians 4:6 says, "Let your speech always be gracious, seasoned with salt." As you progress through this book, season all of your conversations with grace. Be patient with each other, have fun, and enjoy the process. Wishing you many happy conversations in the pages ahead!

Sincerely,

COFFEE SHOP CONVERSATIONS

131
Engaging Conversations
For Couples

*To be fully seen by somebody, then, and be loved
anyhow–this is a human offering that can border
on miraculous.*

~ Elizabeth Gilbert,

*You know you're in love when you can't fall
asleep because reality is finally better than your
dreams.*

~ Dr. Seuss

Two people are better than one.

~ Ecclesiastes 4:9a

Question #1

Imagine that you have the opportunity to grant your partner a superpower. What superhuman ability would you bestow upon him or her, and why?

Question #2

The doctor informs you that you must eliminate either caffeine or sugar from your diet. Which do you get rid of, and why?

Question #3

Describe a happy childhood memory from a camp, trip, or sleepover. Then, share what made this experience so memorable.

Question #4

Similar to the movie *Supersize Me*, you will dine off the menu of a single fast food restaurant for an entire month. Fortunately, you get to choose which eatery this will be. Which restaurant do you select, and why?

Question #5

If you had to relocate to a different state, where would you move, and why?

Question #6

Imagine that you must shut down all of your social media accounts but one. Which accounts would you close? Which site would you continue using? Then, explain why?

Question #7

You have the ability to turn invisible. You can go anywhere, and do anything, completely unseen. How will you use this superpower?

Question #8

Imagine you find a wallet. Inside are a photo identification card and five, $100 bills. No one is around. What will you do with the wallet, i.d. card, and money? Then, explain your reasons behind the decisions you made.

Question #9

Would you rather go skydiving, scuba diving, or relax at home? Why?

Question #10

Complete this sentence, "The three apps on my phone that I can't live without are..."

Question #11

Describe a time during your childhood when you felt especially close to God. Where were you, what happened, and what was this feeling like?

Question #12

What current activities, events, or people help you to feel closer to God?

Question #13

Describe a childhood event that left you with a negative view of God. First, describe what happened, then share how this affected you, personally.

Question #14

Now, describe a current event that left you with a positive view of God. First, tell what happened, and then share how this event contributed to your understanding of God or grew your faith in Him.

Question #15

Imagine, that like in the movie *Groundhog Day*, you will relive the same day, over and over again. What day was so amazing that you would repeat it?

Question #16

George Bernard Shaw said, "If you cannot get rid of the family skeleton, you may as well make it dance." Describe a family skeleton from your childhood.

Question #17

Tell about a time you put Shaw's advice into action and made a family skeleton dance by using a challenge for the good.

Question #18

Describe a current family skeleton. In your opinion, why is this tricky issue hidden away and not talked about openly?

Question #19

What current family skeleton could you creatively use to your advantage? How might you accomplish this?

Question #20

Randy Pausch, the author of *The Last Lecture*,[3] writes, "The brick walls are not there to keep us out. The brick walls are there to give us a chance to show how badly we want something. Because the brick walls are there to stop the people who don't want it badly enough. They're there to stop the other people." Do you agree or disagree with Randy's statement, and why?

Question #21

Describe a time in your life when a brick wall caused you to press forward harder, which led to achieving your goal.

Question #22

Describe a current brick wall you are facing at home, work, or school. How would it feel to overcome this obstacle?

Question #23

What are some ways that your partner can support you in overcoming your current brick wall challenges?

Question #24

When facing the brick walls in your life, would you describe yourself as easily discouraged, someone who persistently presses forward in spite of challenges, or are you somewhere in between? Then, explain why you see yourself this way.

Question #25

In your family, who excels at optimistically pressing forward in the midst of challenging circumstances? What do you think is the secret behind this person's persistence?

Question #26

The Pareto Principle, also known as the 80/20 rule, states that roughly 80% of results come from 20% of our efforts, while 80% of the work we do accounts for a mere 20% of the results. The Pareto Principle is often applied in business, relationships, and life. It is a reminder to focus on the tasks that matter most. Have you heard of this principle before, and what is your overall impression of the concept?

Question #27

In your relationship, what do you consider to be the 20% activities or the ones that draw the two of you the closest together?

Question #28

Complete this sentence, "When you ____, I am blown away by your love for me."

Question #29

Thinking back over your relationship, describe a time when you felt incredibly loved by your partner. What, made this moment so meaningful to you?

Question #30

If your partner wanted to make you feel especially loved today, what types of things should he or she do?

Question #31

According to Pareto, 20% of our daily activities account for nearly 80% of the joy in our life. In regards to happiness, fun, and joy what are some of your 20% activities?

Question #32

When you and your partner are having fun as a couple, what activities bring you the most joy?

Question #33

What are some couples activities that bring you less joy, but that you continue to engage in because you know that it means a lot to your partner?

Question #34

A study reports that some thirteen-year-olds check their social media accounts as much as 100 times a day.[4] How often do you check your social media accounts? How important is social media to your everyday life?

Question #35

Surprise, you are about to contract a mental illness. On the bright side, you get to choose which illness this will be. Which do you pick, and why?

Question #36

Which mental illness frightens you the most, and why?

Question #37

If a loved one suspected you were showing signs of mental illness, how would you want this brought to your attention? How would you want your partner to care for you during this time?

Question #38

Who, in your family, exhibits signs of mental illness? In what ways has this affected your relationship with this person and your life in general?

Question #39

"Trauma is a life-organizing event."[5] This means that painful events from our past can influence the way we interact with others and view the world. Describe a past event that continues to affect you today. Tell what happened, and how the event changed you.

Question #40

Describe someone you know who is stuck in past pain. What do you think caused him or her to get stuck? How are you being an encouragement to this person?

Question #41

Who do you know that has overcome a painful past? What are some of the qualities that might have allowed this person to push past adversity?

Question #42

In regards to trauma, how would you currently describe yourself? Are you stuck in past hurt? Are you in the process of working through the pain, or would you describe yourself as fully recovered from old wounds?

Question #43

If your partner notices that you are having an exceptionally difficult day, how would you want him or her to support you?

Question #44

Children have excellent imaginations. Describe a childhood game or activity that delighted you and your friends.

Question #45

Imagine the pastor of your church asks you to preach a sermon on any topic that you are passionate about. What would the theme of your sermon be?

Question #46

What is one piece of wisdom, given to you by a parent, teacher, coach, or mentor, that has stuck with you over time? Why do you think these words have been so meaningful?

Question #47

Imagine that you are asked to give advice to a newly dating couple. What words of wisdom would you share, and why?

Question #48

When is the last time you laughed aloud, and what made you laugh?

Question #49

Describe something you admire about your grandparents.

Question #50

Describe a quality that you admire in your parents.

Question #51

Most kids try a variety of sports, clubs, and extracurricular activities throughout their childhood. Describe a childhood activity that you gave up, but now wish that you didn't. What was it about this activity that brought you joy?

Question #52

Growing up, what were your biggest pet peeves?

Question #53

Describe your happiest moment over the past week. Why did this moment bring you so much joy?

Question #54

Looking over the past week, describe your greatest disappointment. What made this time so discouraging?

Question #55

Describe a favorite rainy day memory or rainy day activity from childhood.

Question #56

Imagine that you and your partner are stuck indoors during a thunderstorm. Then, describe what the perfect rainy day date would look like.

Question #57

It has been said that "Children may forget what you say, but they will never forget how you made them feel."[6] What childhood mentor, teacher, or friend made you feel especially important?

Question #58

What specific actions do you take to make the people around you feel valued?

Question #59

Describe a time during the past week that your partner made you feel important. What did he or she do, and why did this mean so much to you?

Question #60

If you could travel back in time and witness a Biblical miracle, which miracle would you most like to see?

Question #61

Describe a happy memory from your early twenties. Where were you, who were you with, and what happened?

Question #62

Describe a major disappointment from your early twenties.

Question #63

If you had the opportunity to travel back in time and talk to your twenty-year-old self, what advice would you give?

Question #64

If your twenty-year-old self were to travel into the future and meet you today, what might he or she think? Would your twenty-year-old self be thrilled, disappointed, perplexed, etc.? Why?

Question #65

If you could return to college and study any subject, what would it be, and why?

Question #66

In 2 Peter 3:16, the Apostle Peter states that some things in Scripture are difficult to understand. What is one Biblical concept that confuses or frustrates you?

Question #67

What Biblical passage inspires you the most? Why do these verses mean so much to you, personally?

All you need is love.
But a little chocolate now and then doesn't hurt.

~ Charles Schulz

Question #68

Marriage researcher, John Gottman, writes about the importance of repair attempts, or simple actions that reunite a couple after a quarrel. What repair attempts do you use to reconnect with your partner?

Question #69

How good are you at receiving your partner's repair attempts when he or she tries to reconnect? First, describe what you do well. Then, explain what you could do better.

Question #70

On a scale of 1-10, how good are you and your partner at reconnecting after a disagreement? Then, explain why you assigned this number.

Question #71

What steps could your partner take to make reconnecting after a disagreement easier for you?

Question #72

The next time you are upset, what would you like to do to better manage your feelings of anger, hurt, and sadness?

Question #73

As a child, what did you imagine falling in love would be like?

Question #74

As an adult, how do you know that you are in love?

Question #75

What movie did you dislike so much that you would un-watch it if you could?

Question #76

Imagine a romantic comedy, based on your relationship, is being filmed. The director needs a fresh story for a funny, romantic scene. Which story do you tell?

Question #77

What movie do you consider to be the most romantic movie of all time, and why?

Question #78

A popular axiom proclaims, "A happy wife is a happy life." Do you agree with this statement? Why or why not?

Question #79

Do you believe that the opposite is also true? Does an unhappy wife (or husband) result in an unhappy life? Then, explain your answer.

Question #80

What steps do you take to keep yourself happy throughout the day?

Question #81

How would you like your partner to contribute to your happiness? How good is he or she at doing the things you mentioned?

Question #82

In your opinion, what percentage of your happiness is your responsibility, and what percentage is your partner's responsibility? Then, explain the reasons for the numbers that you gave.

Question #83

Complete this sentence, "In marriage, a husband should always..."

Question #84

Finish this sentence, "In marriage, a husband should never..."

Question #85

Complete this sentence, "In marriage, a wife should always..."

Question #86

Finish this sentence, "In marriage, a wife should never..."

Question #87

Describe how your relationship with your partner has transformed you for the better.

Question #88

Finish this sentence, "If my 16-year-old self were to see me today, he or she would feel proud that..."

Question #89

Who do you consider to be a current mentor or role model? What do you admire about this person?

Question #90

Who are you currently mentoring–or who could you mentor–and what do you think this person could learn from you?

Question #91

What Biblical hero do you greatly admire, and why?

Question #92

What character qualities does this Biblical hero possess, that you would like to emulate?

Question #93

How old were you when you got your first cell phone? Then, tell the story of how you got it.

If you would be loved, love, and be loveable.
~ Benjamin Franklin

Question #94

1 John 4:17, states, "As He (Jesus) is, so are we in this world." How is Christ working through you, as His hands and feet in the world?

Question #95

Who is someone that is acting as Jesus' hands and feet in your life? First, tell who this person is, then share what he or she does that is so meaningful to you.

Question #96

If, you knew that you would lose your ability to hear tomorrow, how would you spend your last day of hearing? Who would you talk with, what songs would you play, etc?

Question #97

What childhood cartoon or toy do you hope comes back in style?

Question #98

What do you consider the hardest thing you ever did? Would ever you do it again?

Question #99

What was your New Year's Resolution for this year, and how much progress have you made toward your goal?

Question #100

Which book, outside of the Bible, has grown your faith the most? What was your biggest take away from this book?

Question #101

In the 2006 comedy, *Click*, Michael Newman, played by Adam Sandler, obtains a universal remote control that allows him to fast-forward through the frustrating parts of his life. If you owned this remote, what parts of your life would you fast-forward through?

Question #102

If you owned a magical remote that allowed you rewind your relationship and change something from the past, what would do differently?

Question #103

Describe a time in your relationship where you wished that you had a magical remote control so that you could push the pause button and cause the moment to stretch out longer. Then, share why this time meant so much to you.

Question #104

In the book *Strength Finder 2.0*, Tom Wrath and Donald Clifton describe how experts excel at their craft by building upon their strengths. What strengths do you see in your partner? These do not need to be the same strengths described in the book but can consist of things that he or she excels at in general.

Question #105

In what ways do your strengths and your partner's strengths complement each other?

Question #106

Describe a time that you and your partner utilized your strengths to successfully navigate a dubious situation.

Question #107

What qualities do you admire most in your partner?

Question #108

Tell a story about something you wanted as a teenager, but were not allowed to have. What was it, why were you not allowed to have it, and what did you do?

Question #109

If you were to start an internet blog, what would you write about, and what would you name your site?

Question #110

What questions have you always wanted to ask your parents, but never did? What kept you from asking?

Question #111

Conversations such as "The birds and the bees," can be difficult for both parents and children. What difficult conversation did your parents not have with you, but you wish they did?

Question #112

Describe one of your partner's quirky habits that you find endearing.

Question #113

What is the most exotic food you have ever tasted, and how did you come about trying it?

Question #114

Tell the story about the time you got in the most trouble as a child.

Question #115

It is said that opposites attract. What are some opposites that attract you to your partner?

Question #116

Tell a story about the worst or most embarrassing date you ever went on. When was it, where did you and your date go, and what happened?

Question #117

Tell the story of how you moved out of your parent's house and began living on your own.

Question #118

What is the biggest adventure you and your best friend had together? Describe where you went and what happened.

Question #119

Tell a story about a recent trip or vacation that did not live up to your expectations. What specifically made this experience so disappointing?

Question #120

Imagine that you have the opportunity to eat lunch with anyone currently living, no matter how famous. Who would you eat with, and what would you talk about?

Question #121

What Biblical character is most like you? In what ways are the two of you alike?

Question #122

What is the best April Fool's joke or practical joke that you ever had played on you?

Question #123

Describe the best prank that you ever pulled on someone else.

Question #124

Describe your motivations for going to work. Is it purely financial, or are there other things that attract you to your job?

Question #125

James 1:2 says to count it all joy when you face trials of all kinds. What trials are you currently facing, and how are you finding joy in the midst of them?

Question #126

What was your favorite book during your teenage years, and what did you love about it?

Question #127

Galatians 5:22-23 says, "The fruit of the Spirit is love, joy, peace, patience, kindness, goodness, faithfulness, gentleness, and self-control." Which fruit do you see in your partner's life, and how do you see them manifest?

Question #128

What spiritual fruits are you producing this year? What steps are you taking to nurture these qualities in your life?

Question #129

What were some of your favorite television shows during middle school, and what did you like about them?

Question #130

What is your favorite nickname, and how did you get it?

Question #131

Now that you have reached the end of this book, how will you continue connecting deeply with your partner?

Creatively Connecting Through Life's Seasons

A friend recently shared how he and his wife spend more time texting than talking. While we both agreed that this is less than ideal, it is also not awful either. This particular friend, like so many people I know, is going through an extraordinarily busy season of life. The bright side is that amidst all of the hustle and bustle, texting keeps him and his wife connected.

I once heard about a Navy Seal, who would write short love notes to his wife, on postcard size paper. He would hide these letters around the house before long deployments, and his wife would discover them over time. This simple idea is creative and ingenious. It is another example of how happy couples connect during busy seasons.

Finally, there is the egg story. Because I heard it many years ago, I only remember a few of the details. The speaker shared how he once wrote short love messages to his wife on every egg in the carton. I don't remember exactly why he did this. There may have been a special occasion involved, or it might have been purely spontaneous. What I do remember is thinking to myself, "One day, after I am married, I am going to try this!" While I have not done this yet, the idea is in my repertoire of creative connection ideas.

I share these simple stories because they illustrate two important points. First, they show how connecting does not need to be difficult, expensive, or time-consuming. Connecting does not require sending a hundred roses to our loved one's work on Valentine's Day. It can be as simple as giving our partner one rose, on any ordinary day of the week, and doing it simply because connecting for a moment is important.

Second, these stories demonstrate that connecting can be fun. Each story gets progressively more outrageous, and this is how it should be. Connecting is not a task to be completed, nor is it one more item to check off a list. Connecting is more like breathing and blinking, we do it because it is in our genes.

God has hardwired you and me to connect. During some seasons of life, this will be easy. During other seasons, an extra dose of creativity will be required. The important thing is to connect often, connect intimately, and to reconnect quickly every time a disruption occurs.

For you and your partner, accomplishing this might involve diving into another book of conversation starters, sending multiple texts to each other throughout the day, hiding love notes all over your home, or creatively decorating each egg in the carton with loving words of affirmation. The most important thing is to stay connected throughout every season of life.

Wishing you many seasons of creative connecting in the years ahead!

End Notes

1. Genesis 2:18

2. Gottman, John and Silver, Nan. *The Seven Principles for Making Marriage Work: A Practical Guide from the Country's Foremost Relationship Expert*, Harmony Publisher, 2015.

3. Pausch, Randy. *The Last Lecture*, Hyperion Publisher, 2008.

4. Wallace, Kelly. CNN, *Teens spend a 'mind-boggling' 9 hours a day using media, report says. November 3, 2013.* http://www.cnn.com/2015/11/03/health/teens-tweens-media-screen-use-report/

5. A quote from Pam Wright, spoken at a conference on the long-term effects of trauma, recalled from memory.

6. A variation of a quote attributed to Carol Buchner, Maya Angelou, and others.

131
Necessary Conversations
Before Marriage

Insightful, highly-caffeinated,
Christ-honoring conversation starters
for dating and engaged couples!

Jed Jurchenko

www.CoffeeShopConversations.com

Introduction

"Some couples put more effort into researching their next vehicle purchase than in getting to know their future spouse."[1] A favorite psychology professor repeated this statement throughout my stint in graduate school. I and the rest of the class would chuckle. The quote has a sarcastic, pessimistic, and outright comical ring to it. *This is simply too absurd to be true,* I thought to myself.

Fast-forward ten years. I am a licensed marriage and family therapist and regularly rub shoulders with other professionals in my field. In addition to providing guidance to my clients, I also glean from their stories, while continuing to amass valuable life experience of my own. It is astounding how much personal growth a decade brings! As a result of these experiences, I have concluded—that in spite of its humorous undertones—my professor's declaration is no joke.

A number of key events contributed to this shift in view. First, there are the horror stories recounted by fellow therapists. One colleague described how a couple entered premarital counseling only to discover that while she fervently desires children, he has no interest whatsoever. Even after years of dating and their engagement, this couple never broached this necessary subject!

Then, there is a story from my time serving as a children's pastor. The engaged couple were longtime church members, who were well liked by the pastoral staff. Shortly after the wedding, the husband returned from work to find his bride passed out, drunk. He was utterly shocked. Yet, further conversations with her side of the family revealed that this was a typical pattern of behavior. This new husband had no idea that she was a functional alcoholic until after they walked down the aisle! As you have probably guessed, my friend's marriage did not last. Equally as distressing is the fact that this man's account is not an oddity. Love stories that spiral into disaster are the reason the phrase, "Love is blind," is so common.

Finally, there is the story of my own failed marriage. I hesitate to include this example because I wish it were not the case. I would like to tell you that my story is smooth and clean, but that would be dishonest. During my first engagement, I was naive. I enthusiastically listened with my ears as all of the right answers were uttered. Regrettably, I failed to watch with my eyes and to pay attention to that gut feeling that warns when danger is on the horizon. Had I listened at this intense level, I would have understood that the words spoken were not in alignment with my future bride's actions. Sadly, I too became a casualty of blind love.

The Happy Marriage Myth

The idea that true love is the only necessary ingredient for a life of "happily ever after," is a well-rehearsed marriage myth. Walking down the aisle, then driving off to a life of endless bliss only happens in fairytales. The truth is that a happy union requires ongoing, intentional investments and lots of hard work. Love alone—even powerful love—is not a permanent glue that holds a couple together.

In fact, after a couple ties the knot is when the real undertakings begin. Matrimony may be the grandest personal development course that life has to offer. The good news is that although an excellent marriage requires continual effort, it can also be incredibly fun! I can attest to this because I grew from my past mistakes.

New Beginnings

I knew there was something incredible about Jenny from our very first date. Her gentle smile, compassionate spirit, and the way she insisted that we continue our bayside stroll even after the frigid night air rolled in, instantly won me over. It took me weeks to muster up the courage to ask Jenny for a second date—I was that nervous! My mind whirled a mile a minute as I realized how easy it would be to fall in love with this remarkable woman, and I was not sure that I was ready.

Fortunately, Jenny is patient and was not disheartened by my slow pace. She and I dated for six months before I introduced her to my parents and two daughters. After this,

Jenny, the girls, and I began attending church together every Sunday. We spent plenty of time together during the rest of the week too. Then, following a year-and-a-half of dating—after going through questions books similar to this one, listening to Jenny's words and observing her actions, after an abundance of laughter, countless date-night adventures, and concluding that Jenny was the person I longed to do life with—I popped the question.

Jenny replied with a resounding "yes," and I was ecstatic! In spite of being convinced that the two of us were meant to be, Jenny and I spent another thirteen months planning, preparing, and continuing to get to know one another before sealing the deal with the words, "I do."

Four years have passed since that glorious day. Marriage is not always easy, but it is extraordinarily good. While our blended family does not have a fairytale ending—or if such an ending exists, we have yet to find it—there is a deep-rooted contentment that persists through every storm that life sends our way. This joy comes from knowing that Jenny and I are on one another's side and that each of us has the other's best interest at heart. The two of us readily agree that the scores of challenges we have faced have ultimately served to draw us closer. Most importantly, Jenny and I are best friends who truly enjoy being in each other's presence.

Marital Crash Test Dummies

A few years ago, I accompanied a group of teens to a maximum-security prison. After undergoing a thorough search, we were ushered into a cramped conference room. A guard firmly stationed himself in front of the exit. Then, a line of lifers—convicts with a life sentence, who demonstrated exceptional behavior and a desire to reach out to troubled teens—filed into the room. One by one, each man took his turn at the microphone and shared the story of his dubious past.

The presentation was as professional as any I have seen. These men commanded respect, connected with their audience, and an intense stillness washed over the room.

The session concluded with one inmate pleading with the youth, "Let us be the crash-test dummies. You are here because you are going down the same destructive path we did, but trust me; you do not want to end up like us. Learn from our errors, and do not make the same mistakes."

I want to make a similar plea to you. Let other couples be the marital crash-test dummies. Learn from the many miserable marriages and incredible unions that have come before yours. As you work through the 131 conversations in this book, listen to your partner with your ears, eyes, gut, and heart. Give a hundred times more attention to knowing your spouse than you would to purchasing your next vehicle. Choose wisely. Then, enjoy every moment of your incredible journey together!

Choosing Well

An occupational hazard of being a therapist is the many stories of positive and negative therapeutic experiences that come your way. Nearly everyone has an impassioned story to tell. One couple recounted how, during premarital sessions, the therapist stated he would try to break up their engagement. The reasoning behind this approach was the idea that if the relationship could withstand the pre-marital sessions, then it could survive anything. Rest assured, I do not prescribe to this goofy logic.

The aim of this book is neither to encourage nor to discourage your marriage. Instead, my goal is to facilitate insightful and necessary conversations that will allow you to make an informed decision. There are a number of reasons for this. The first is to encourage you and your partner to invest in meaningful conversations that you might not have thought of on your own.

A second goal of this book is to give you permission to ask. You will not find R-rated questions in this book, nor inquires written with the intention of embarrassing anyone. My hope is that these conversation starters make asking the difficult questions—the ones that need to be raised before the wedding—easier. This is a vital step in assuring that the two of you do not become another casualty of blind love.

While dating, Jenny and I worked through a number of conversation books similar to this one. The two of us took turns asking questions in coffee shops, during walks on the beach, and picnics in the park. Not only did we get to know each other exceedingly well, it also created an abundance of happy memories that we cherish to this day. This is my final reason for writing this book. My hope is that these conversations generate a multitude of joyful memories in the days ahead.

Trusting the Process

"Trust the process," is another favorite axiom of my graduate school professor and a concluding piece of wisdom in this introduction. As you work through these 131 conversations, commit to slowing down and trusting the process. Do this by creating follow-up questions of your own, answering your partner authentically, and enjoying every moment to the fullest! Allowing these conversations to be a process is what leads to relationship intimacy.

I define intimacy as in-to-me-see. It is the ability to know another person while simultaneously being known. Intimacy involves a mutual sharing of inner-worlds, including hopes, hurts, dreams, and nightmares. This process of mutual sharing binds hearts together.

Jenny and I know each other better than anyone else does, and we love each other as is—shining successes, dismal failures, and all. My prayer is that this book aids you on your journey toward this deep-rooted, relational joy. So grab a cup of coffee, tea, or other favorite beverage and dive in!

Sincerely,

COFFEE SHOP CONVERSATIONS

Seven Habits of
Miserable Couples

Learn to recognize these miserable habits.
Then, avoid them as you would a rabid dog.

Neither happy relationships, nor miserable marriages happen by accident. Both are the result of habits. Happy couples consistently engage in the types of actions that happy couples take. If you and your spouse behave in the ways that happy couples do, soon the feelings will follow. The key to becoming–and staying–a happy couple is to develop healthy, happy habits.

Of course, the opposite is equally as true. Miserable couples behave in the ways that miserable couples do. In other words, misery in marriage also has a predictable and well-worn path. It really is that simple!

This chapter outlines seven, deadly relationship habits. As you read this list, take mental notes of any destructive habits infesting your relationship. Then, team-up with your partner to exterminate them. One of the easiest ways to accomplish this is to replace the negative habit with a positive one–such as one of the habits found in the next chapter, which hones in on the seven habits of happy couples. The routines you and your partner practice on a daily basis will make or break your marriage.

The Seven Habits of Miserable Couples

1. Miserable couples criticize often.

Criticism is an attack on the other person's character. Instead of saying, "You made a mistake," criticism says, "You are the mistake!" According to relationship expert John Gottman, criticism is not only a marriage killer, it is so deadly that he refers to it as one of, "The Four Horsemen of the Apocalypse."[2] While marital disagreements are normal, healthy part of relationships, attacking your spouse's character is poison.

2. Miserable couples point in blame.

Blaming says, "You caused the problem, and you need to fix it." Because blaming demands the other person take full responsibility for the issue at hand, it obliterates opportunities for collaboration and teamwork. According to Scripture, marriage joins two people together as one. Blaming is deadly because it is a direct attack on attack marital oneness, and this does neither spouse any good.

3. Miserable couples complain.

Complaining is deadly because it magnifies the problem. In fact, the more a couple complains, the bigger the problem appears. There is a big difference between venting and brainstorming solutions in a reasonable manner. The first adds to the problem while the second seeks to resolve them. Complaining is deadly because it does not seek resolution.

Studies—such as the BoBo Doll experiment—reveal that venting is highly contagious.[3] In this experiment, children observed adults hit and toss around a blow-up BoBo doll through a small window. Next, the child entered the room. The child would naturally reenact the observed behaviors with no prompting required. Parental modeling is powerful! Children soak up negative interactions like a dry sponge, and then repeat these patterns in their own relationships.

4. Miserable couples nag.

Nagging is a leaky faucet. Proverbs 27:16 says, "A continual dripping on a rainy day and a contentious wife are alike." There is no doubt in my mind that the same is true for a contentious husband. Do not allow your relationship to die the death of a thousand, icy drips. Tighten the faucet of your lips by turning off nagging in your home.

5. Miserable couples make threats.

Threats are especially problematic because they create a catch-22 situation. If the threatened spouse concedes by changing, the threatened spouse is sure to face similar threats in future—likely the next time the couple reaches an impasse. If the spouse holds firm in the face of peril, and the threat acted upon, additional negativity enters into the relationship. Nothing good ever comes from threats.

6. Miserable couples punish.

Couples who punish build their relationship on fear. Before punishing ask yourself, "Why would I want to hurt the person I love?"Obviously, there is no good reason to do this. Ultimately, punishments hurt the relationship.

7. Miserable couples bribe to get their way.

Although bribes are more appealing than threats and punishments, they are one more form of coercion. Bribing is one more attempt to get one's spouse to do something that he or she is opposed to doing.

Perhaps you have noticed the common theme running through these seven habits. Miserable couples seek to control, manipulate, and change their partner. As you work through this book, if there are things about your partner that you simply cannot accept, make a firm commitment to work through these issues before your wedding day.

Change is tricky, and most couples argue about the same problems throughout the course of their marriage. In my opinion, it is far better to accept your spouse as he or she is or to decide to break-up prior to the marriage, than to argue back and forth for the remainder of your days on earth.

Happy Couples vs. Miserable Couples

Happy couples team-up. They work together to find win-win solutions. In a happy relationship, partners change out of love for their spouse, but compliance is not demanded.

On the other hand, miserable couples put forth great efforts to force change. There is little patience and no room for individual differences. The renowned psychologist William Glasser called these attempts to control our loved ones, *external control psychology*. Each of the seven habits of miserable couples is an external control psychology tactic.

Scripture opposes eternal control psychology in marriage. One example of this is in Philippians 2:4, which states "Let each of you look not only to his own interests but also to the interests of others." Miserable couples can move toward a more joyful relationship by putting this Scripture into action.

Now that you know the seven habits of miserable couples, avoid them with gusto. The bottom line is that miserable couples follow a well-trodden path of miserable behaviors, while happy couples conduct themselves in an equally predictable pattern of happiness. In the next chapter, you will learn seven habits of happy couples. Then, act the way that happy couples do!

Warm-up Conversations

Have you and your partner ever fallen into one of the miserable couples traps? If so, which ones?

Next time you and your partner begin acting the ways that miserable couples do, what will each of you do differently?

When your spouse catches you engaging in one of these miserable patterns of behavior, how would you like him or her to bring it to your attention?

Seven Habits of Happy Couples

Essential, happy habits to keep your spouse's love-bank full!

It was a lazy Saturday afternoon. I was in my mid-twenties and lived in a one-bedroom condominium that I had recently purchased. I don't remember why I was rummaging through the junk drawer in my kitchen. I may have been cleaning, or I could have been looking for something I had lost. What I do remember is the feeling of horror that washed over me in the moments that followed.

As I fumbled through the drawer, I found two checkbooks from separate banks. *This is odd*, I thought to myself. Upon closer examination, I realized that one checkbook was linked to my current bank, while the second was connected to an account I had closed a few months prior.

The smart decision would have been to immediately dispose of the old checks after closing the account. Regrettably, I overlooked this step, and I bet you can guess which account I had written checks out of all week. My heart leaped into my throat, and I felt my face flush with a mixture of embarrassment and anxiety as I grasped the magnitude of my blunder.

How could someone responsible enough to buy his own condo make such an egregious error? I silently wondered. This particular bank charged a hefty fee for every over-draft purchase. I wrote seven checks from this closed account, and knew I was in trouble!

Fixing Mistakes

My lazy, Saturday afternoon turned into a scramble. I darted to the bank, explained my predicament, and fortunately, was able to reinstate my old account before too much damage occurred.

To this day, I remember the gut-wrenching terror that swept over me after discovering I wrote checks from a closed account. It is an experience I hope to never repeat.

Yet, as bad as having an overdrawn bank account is, overdrawing from our spouse's love-bank is far worse. According to *Stepfamily.org*, one out of two marriages ends in divorce, and the average marriage only lasts seven years.[4] Prior to divorce come feelings of emptiness, hurt, anger, and despair. Divorce is rarely a sudden act. More often, it is the final destination couples who have amassed a gaping love-debt.

The Love Bank Secret

Happy couples keep each other's love-bank filled to the brim. The secret to accomplishing this does not stem from massive, one-time love-bank deposits. Instead, happy couples make many smaller deposits daily. Exotic vacations and extravagant acts are added bonuses to an already thriving marriage. This chapter outlines seven habits that will assist you in making love-deposits daily.

Each habit is founded on solid psychological principles and aligns with a Biblical worldview. I have a friend who likes to say "God said it first," because the best techniques that psychology offers are usually a rediscovery of Biblical principles that have been ignored. Listed below, you will find the seven, love bank-filling habits, of happy couples, along with Scriptures that highlight the importance of each one.

Seven Habits of Happy Couples

1. Happy couples support each other.

Happy couples strive to be one another's biggest fans. Hebrews 10:24 says, "Let us take thought of how to spur one another on to love and good works." While it is possible to overdo appreciation, this rarely happens. As a marriage and family therapist, I have never seen—nor heard of—a partner complaining, "My spouse appreciates me too much." So, make your praise sincere, and voice your appreciation often.

2. Happy couples encourage.

Ephesians 4:29 says, "You must let no unwholesome word come out of your mouth, but only what is beneficial for the building up of the one in need." Our souls thirst for encouragement as a tree longs for water. For a deep-rooted, flourishing marriage, encourage your spouse daily.

3. Happy couples listen with their entire being.

Listening is more than parroting back the last words that fell from your spouse's lips. Heartfelt hearing requires engaged effort. Couples who practice this habit put James 1:19 into action. This passage says, "Let every person be quick to listen, slow to speak, slow to anger." God gave us two ears and one mouth for a reason. Striving to listen to our spouse twice as much as we speak is a good place to begin.

4. Happy Couples accept each other's flaws and strengths.

When others accept our weaknesses, we are better able to move on. Surprisingly, the act of acceptance—and not blaming and shaming—is precisely what opens the door to dynamic change and growth. Acceptance is a principle modeled by Christ Himself. Romans 5:8 says, "But God demonstrates his own love for us in this: While we were still sinners, Christ died for us." God accepts you as you are, warts and all. Happy couples follow His lead by accepting our spouse where he or she is at and allowing change to flow naturally, over time.

5. Happy couples build trust daily.

Proverbs 28:20 says, "A faithful person will have an abundance of blessings." Happy couples fill each other's love-banks by being faithful in the little things. It is during the ordinary days of marriage that extraordinary trust is developed. In short, faithfulness builds trust, and trust is the foundation of a happy marriage!

6. Happy couples demonstrate respect.

Ephesians 5:33, proclaims the value of love and respect within marriage and is the foundational Scripture in the book, *Love and Respect*.[5] Author Emerson Eggerichs proposes that men thrive in relationships where respect is shown. As someone who has been a part of countless men's groups and a member of the male species myself, I can attest that respect is an especially big deal for guys.

7. Happy couples negotiate differences.

Proverbs 21:9 states, "It is better to live on a corner of the housetop than in a house in company with a quarrelsome wife." I am sure that the same thing is true for a quarrelsome husband.

In college, therapists discuss the pursue-flee dynamic. This harmful pattern occurs when one partner—who longs for the conflict to end—flees, while the other—desperate to bring resolution to the conflict—responds in pursuit. Although the motives of each may be pure, the results are never pretty. Instead of getting stuck in this chaotic relationship dynamic, find a way to negotiate differences, and move on.

Creating Win-Win Solutions

You have probably noticed that the seven qualities of happy couples are not one-time strategies, but ongoing attitudes. Couples who integrate these habits into their lives are making continual deposits into their spouse's love-bank. This is the best way to make sure one's account is never overdrawn.

Warm-up Conversations

Which love-bank filling habits are you already practicing?

Which happy habits are an area of growth for you and your partner?

Which happy habit fills your own love-bank the most?

When I feel like my love bank is nearing empty, how would you like me to let you know?

131 Necessary Conversations Before Marriage

Chains do not hold marriage together.
It is threads, hundreds of tiny threads which
sew people together through the years.

~ Simone Signoret

And the two will become one flesh.
So they are no longer two, but one flesh.

~ Mark 10:8

Conversation #1

Imagine that a well-known Hollywood producer wants to make a movie about your relationship and you get to choose the actors. Whom would you select to star as you and your partner? Why?

Conversation #2

If you could travel back in time and relive a part of your relationship, what would it be? What things would you do differently, and what would you keep the same?

Conversation #3

If your loved one wanted to surprise you with your favorite meal, what should he or she cook?

Conversation #4

Describe, in detail, your idea of a perfect romantic evening.

Conversation #5

What small gestures of love are the most meaningful to you? Why?

Conversation #6

How do you think that married life will differ from your single life?

Conversation #7

When you were growing up, what did arguments look like in your home?

Conversation #8

When it comes to disagreements, what do you plan on doing similarly to your parents and what will you do differently?

Conversation #9

What are some of your favorite hobbies and free-time activities?

Conversation #10

Which hobbies and activities will you expect your spouse to participate in with you? How does he or she feel about this?

Conversation #11

How do you think your hobbies will change after marriage? In what ways will they stay the same?

Conversation #12

In your opinion, what are three things that make your partner attractive?

Conversation #13

Why do you want to get married and why do you want to marry your partner?

Conversation #14

Describe a time the two of you navigated a disagreement successfully. What skills did you use that worked well?

Conversation #15

Think back to one of your more challenging conflicts. What made this disagreement so difficult, and is there anything that you wish you had done differently?

Conversation #16

During a presidential election, would you more likely to vote for a candidate with the greatest political experience or the candidate with the strongest moral values? Why?

Conversation #17

Which political party do you most closely associate with, and why?

Conversation #18

Does it make any difference to you which political party your spouse endorses? Why or why not?

Conversation #19

Do you want to have children? Why or why not?

Conversation #20

If you plan to have children, how many kids would you like to have, and when would you like to have your first child?

Conversation #21

In your opinion, what are the most important values that parents can teach their children?

True love stories never have endings.

~ Richard Bach

Conversation #22

What is your favorite holiday and how do you celebrate it?

Conversation #23

Are there any holidays that you don't celebrate? If so, why not?

Conversation #24

Do you prescribe to a particular faith? If so, on a scale of 1-10, how important is your faith to you? (1 is not very important and 10 is incredibly important.)

Conversation #25

Does it matter if your partner shares your faith or values? Why or why not?

Conversation #26

Growing up, what faith-based traditions were important in your family? (For example, did you attend church weekly, go through confirmation, get baptized, pray before meals, etc.)

Conversation #27

What role will faith play in your new family, and will this role change when you have children?

Conversation #28

What kind of discipline was implemented in your home when you were a child?

Conversation #29

When you have children, what will discipline look like in your new family, and who will be responsible for implementing it?

Conversation #30

Who are some of your closest friends and why are these friendships important to you?

Conversation #31

How will your relationships with your friends change after you are married?

Conversation #32

How many credit cards do you have, and what is your total credit card debt?

Conversation #33

When it comes to finances, do you consider yourself more of a saver or more of a spender? As a bonus, tell a story that illustrates your saving and spending habits.

Conversation #34

Growing up, what were your parent's views toward money? Were they more likely to save, spend, plan, etc.?

Conversation #35

How will your new family manage money similarly and differently than your parents did?

Conversation #36

Will the two of you have separate or joint bank accounts? Why?

Conversation #37

What types of purchases will you and your spouse talk about beforehand, and which purchases will you make without prior discussion?

Conversation #38

Once you are married, where will the two of you live?

Conversation #39

Would you ever consider living in a different state or country? For what reasons would you be willing to move?

Conversation #40

Describe your ideal home using as much detail as you can. Where is it located? How many rooms are there? What is the yard like? Etc.

Conversation #41

Do you plan to attend college or trade school in the future? If so, how does your partner feel about this?

Conversation #42

Who is the happiest couple that you know? In your opinion, what makes this couple's relationship work so well?

Conversation #43

On a scale of 1-10, with 1 being miserable and 10 being ecstatic, how happy are you at your present job? Why?

Conversation #44

Where do you picture yourself working 10 years from now?

Conversation #45

Imagine you peer into a crystal ball and see a glimpse of your family ten years in the future. Describe what you see.

Conversation #46

In regards to roles and responsibilities at home, what would you do similarly to your family of origin and what things would you like to do differently?

Conversation #47

Growing up, what household tasks did your dad take responsibility for and which did your mom do? How well did these family roles work for them?

Conversation #48

What do you think are the key ingredients necessary for a lifetime of love?

Conversation #49

Do you believe in traditional or non-traditional gender-roles in the home? For example, would you want the husband to work, while the wife takes the primary role in raising the children or vice versa?

Conversation #50

How are you and your partner currently modeling these key ingredients of love (described in the previous question) in your relationship?

Conversation #51

In your opinion, is divorce ever justified? If so, what would be viable reasons for getting a divorce?

Conversation #52

What is a favorite holiday memory that you and your partner have together? What makes this memory so special to you?

Conversation #53

After marriage, how will you divide the holidays between your families? Will you celebrate alone as a couple, with one or both sets of parents, create a rotating schedule, etc.?

Conversation #54

What is a favorite memory of a family vacation?

Conversation #55

What types of vacations do you hope to take in the future?

Conversation #56

Do you see yourself always working, being a homemaker, or retiring early? How does your partner feel about this?

Conversation #57

Are there any household tasks such as cooking, laundry, paying bills, etc. that you do not do, either because you choose not to do them or because you don't know how to do them?

Conversation #57

Do you consider yourself a morning person or a night person? If you and your spouse differ, how might you navigate this?

Conversation #58

Do you like to keep your home clean and organized, or are you fine with a creative mess?

Conversation #59

Do you consider yourself an affectionate person? Why or why not?

Conversation #60

They say, "Opposites attract." What are some opposites that you find attractive in your partner?

Conversation #61

What are some differences your partner has that you find annoying? How will the two of you negotiate these differences?

Love one another and you will be happy.
It's as simple and as difficult as that.
. ~Micheal Leunig

Conversation #62

If there were an unexpected pregnancy, would you or your spouse ever consider an abortion? Why or why not?

Conversation #63

According to statistics, nearly half of first marriages end in divorce. Why do you think this is the case?

Conversation #64

What are some reasons that your marriage will succeed? (You may want to team-up and list ten reasons that your marriage will defy the odds.)

Conversation #65

When you and your spouse go through challenging times, whom will you look to for wisdom and support?

Conversation #66

Imagine you are having a horrendous day. How would you like your spouse to comfort and encourage you?

Conversation #67

Once married, will you share email and social media accounts or keep them separate? Why?

Conversation #68

What is one of your favorite nonfiction books, and what was your biggest take away from the book?

Conversation #69

What is a favorite fiction book? What was it about the story that caught your interest?

Conversation #70

If your relationship was a book, what section of the bookstore would it be placed in, and why? (For example, drama, comedy, steamy romance, tragedy, etc.)

Conversation #71

What is something that you are doing to grow as a person this year?

For it was not into my ear you whispered,
but into my heart.
~Judy Garland

Conversation #72

How would you like your partner to support you in your personal growth?

Conversation #73

Have you ever used drugs recreationally (including marijuana and prescription pills), and what is your current attitude toward recreational drug use?

Conversation #74

Growing up, what was your parent's attitude toward alcohol? (Were they teetotalers, casual drinkers, alcoholics, in recovery, etc?)

Conversation #75

What will the attitude toward alcohol be in your new home?

Conversation #76

What is the most you ever drank in a day? What, if anything, did you learn from the experience?

Conversation #77

When you feel stressed out, what helps you to relax?

Conversation #78

On a scale of 1-10, how adventurous are you? A 1 means "Watching *The Discovery Chanel,* on t.v. is as adventurous as it gets." A 10 means, "Skydiving, chocolate covered bacon, and scuba diving, I'll do it all!"

Conversation #79

What has been one of your favorite adventures together so far, and what made this time so special?

Conversation #80

What adventures would you like to have with your future spouse?

Conversation #81

What television series are you currently watching, and what do you like about it?

Love is the master key
that opens the gates of happiness.
~ Oliver Wendell Holmes

Conversation #82

When you were a child, what were some of the house rules?

Conversation #83

What is one rule that was helpful, and what is one rule that could have been better?

Conversation #84

What are some house rules you hope to implement in your own home—both immediately and after you have children?

Conversation #85

When you are sick, how would you like your spouse to care for you?

Conversation #86

What has been one of your favorite romantic dates together so far? What made this time so meaningful?

Conversation #87

What are some of the relationship skills you are using to make your friendship work well?

Conversation #88

What are some of the best ways your partner shows you that he or she cares?

Conversation #89

Are there any lingering physical or mental health issues that you have not told your spouse about? If so, what are they?

Conversation #90

Have you ever been arrested? If so, what is the story behind the arrest, and what did you learn from it?

Conversation #91

Growing up, how often did your family attend church services together?

Conversation #92

How often will the two of you attend church once you are married?

Conversation #93

If Jesus were to ask you, "Who do you say that I am?" How would you answer, and why?

Conversation #94

Every family has a unique culture in their home. Describe what your family culture was like when you were growing up?

Conversation #95

What would you like your new family culture to be like? In what ways will it be similar to your old family culture and in how will it differ?

Conversation #96

On a scale of 1-10, how happy are you with your physical appearance, and why?

Conversation #97

If you could change one thing about your physical appearance, what would it be, and why?

Conversation #98

If you and your spouse were in an especially rough patch in your marriage, would you be willing to attend couples counseling? Why or why not?

Conversation #99

What is the worst injury you ever had, and how did it happen?

Conversation #100

Will you continue to stay in contact with old girlfriends or boyfriends after you are married? How does your partner feel about this?

Conversation #101

What are a few of life's simple pleasures that bring you joy?

Conversation #102

Growing up, how were problems addressed in your family? Were they ignored, shouted, discussed, etc.

Conversation #103

What would make it difficult for you to share a current problem with your spouse?

Conversation #104

What do you picture your relationship with your new in-laws being like?

Conversation #105

What do you picture your relationship with your new in-laws being like?

Conversation #106

Describe what your ideal wedding day looks like?

Conversation #107

Imagine that you find a magic lamp on your wedding day. The genie inside offers to grant you three wishes for your marriage. Working together, what do you and your spouse wish for?

Conversation #108

If you knew that you were about to be stranded on a deserted island, and had the opportunity to take one luxury item with you, what would you bring?

Conversation #109

In your opinion, how important is the wedding day to your overall relationship? Does an amazing wedding create a better marriage?

Conversation #110

Would you rather have a large wedding or a small wedding? Why?

Conversation #111

How important is the wedding day to you personally, and why?

Conversation #112

What spiritual activities will the two of you engage in as a couple?

Conversation #113

Describe a time when God answered your prayer. What did you pray for, and how did God provide?

Conversation #114

When was the last time you prayed, and what did you pray about?

Conversation #115

What are some ways that your partner can pray for you?

Conversation #116

What song best describes your relationship and why?

Conversation #117

Do you ever lay awake at night worried? If so, what causes you to stress?

Conversation #118

What character qualities do you find especially attractive in your loved one, and why?

Conversation #1119

On a scale of 1-10, how much do you enjoy spending time with your spouse's friends? A 10 means, "I love it. They are the best!" A 1 means, "Help! Get me away from these crazy people, please!"

Conversation #120

What is one quote, or piece of advice that you try to live by? Why does this statement resonate with you?

Conversation #121

If you could travel back in time and ask one Biblical figure for marriage advice, who would you meet with and what would you ask?

Conversation #122

If you could travel back in time and ask one historical figure (outside of the Bible) for marriage advice, who would you meet with and what would you ask?

Conversation #123

What makes you nervous about marriage?

Conversation #124

What gets you excited about being married?

Conversation #125

What was your favorite childhood pet, and what is a favorite pet memory?

Conversation #126

Would you ever want to own a pet or pets? If so, what kind and how many?

Conversation #127

Describe your favorite Christmas traditions? Which ones do you plan to carry over into your new family?

Conversation #128

Describe some of your favorite Thanksgiving traditions? Which ones do you plan to carry over into your new family?

Conversation #129

Do you find it easy or difficult to be thankful? Why do you think this is?

Conversation #130

What is the most important or most insightful thing you learned about your partner while going through the questions in this book?

Conversation #131

Now that you have completed these questions, what will you do to continue to learn about your partner and foster a spirit of in-to-me-see as a couple?

Seven Habits for After Tying the Knot

Happy habits for a vibrant marriage!

Happy couples keep the loving actions going after they are married. Sometimes, when my younger brother asks me what my plans are for the weekend, I jokingly reply, "I'm going to lay on the couch, watch action movies, and eat junk-food all weekend long. I've attracted my wife, so there is no reason to stay in shape, or to go out anymore." Before judging me too harshly, rest assured that this is not something I would actually do.

I love spending time with Jenny and our daughters. In fact, it is my absolute favorite thing to do! A day at the beach walks to the park, and family meals are far more appealing to me than zoning-out in front of the television. I am well aware that happily married couples continue to actively engage in the happy marriage habits they created before the wedding.

Sadly, there are couples who live out my sarcastic joke. This final chapter is a gentle reminder to keep love going after tying the knot.

Seven Habits for After Tying the Knot

1. Keep putting your best foot forward.

While dating, couples are on their best behavior. They listen attentively, laugh at each other's jokes, and choose to believe the best about each other. Married couples tend to be more honest, raw, and real. While this can be good–because raw emotions and serious conversation adds much to the relationship–don't forget to put your best foot forward too. Marriage is not an excuse for relational laziness. Happy couples put their best foot forward, day after day.

2. Catch foxes.

Song of Solomon 2:15 says, "Catch for us the foxes, the little foxes that ruin the vineyards, our vineyards that are in bloom." "Catch the little foxes," is another way of saying, "Let the little things go." Tiny foxes ruin a vineyard, and small grudges fester and spoil a marriage. The second happy marriage habit is to choose to see the best in your spouse by letting the small stuff go!

3. Have fun.

Dating is fun, and marriage needs to be fun too. Don't stop laughing, joking, and having fun together after the wedding. Marriage does not need to be fun all of the time, but it must be fun some of the time. What actions are you taking to keep the joy in your relationship alive?

4. Keep saying, "I love you."

I once heard a story about a wife who asked her husband, "Do you still love me?" The husband replied, "Honey, I told you I loved you on our wedding day, and if anything changes, I will let you know." Do not be this couple!

Proclamations of "I love you," should abound, along with plenty of words of affirmation, and caring actions to back them up. While it is true that love is a verb that must be demonstrated with actions, the vocabulary is still essential. Refine the art of speaking and demonstrating love in your relationship.

5. Fill your spouse's love-bank daily.

Imagine a rich uncle offers you a gift of a million dollars today, or the gift of a penny a day, doubled every day, for the next thirty days. Which would you choose?

If you have heard this before–or if you took the time to do the math–then you know to go for the penny. A penny a day, doubled every day, for thirty days, starts small. However, by day thirty, you would receive $5,368,709.10. When you add this to what you collected over the previous twenty-nine days, you have amassed the grand total of $10,737,418.23. The point of the story is that small investments compound over time and produce big results. This is true in finances and it is true with love. Make small love investments daily and watch your love grow over time.

6. Keep dating.

Dating is more challenging after marriage and even more so after children. However, do not let this stop you. Difficulties only mean that more creativity is required. Set a regular date night, find a good babysitter, and learn how to engage in date night activities after the kiddos have gone to bed—because after kids, sometimes a night on the town simply takes up too much energy. With creativity and practice, dating can be even more fun after the wedding!

7. Ask good questions.

Happy couples stay curious. Remember, intimacy is in-to-me-see. You and your spouse are continually changing. There will always be new things to learn about each other. So, keep talking and stay curious. May your marriage overflow with happiness and love in the years ahead!

Concluding Conversations

Which of these happy marriage habits are you good at?

Which habits do you need to continue growing in?

Are there any habits you would add to this list?

End Notes

1. Quote credited to Dr. Barry Lord.

2. Gottman, John and Silver, Nan. *The Seven Principles For Making Marriage Work*, Harmony, 2015.

3. Information on this popular experiment is readily available. You can find more on Wikepedia at: https://en.wikipedia.org/wiki/Bobo_doll _experiment

4. *Step Family Statics. Retrieved from:* http://www.stepfamily.org/stepfamily-statistics.html

5. Eggerich, Emerson. *Love and Respect*, *Thomas Nelson, 2004.*

Thumbs Up
or Thumbs Down

THANK YOU for purchasing this book!

I would love to hear from you! Your feedback not only helps me grow as a writer, it also helps me to get books into the hands of those who need them most. Online reviews are one of the biggest ways that independent authors—like me—connect with new readers.

If you loved the book, could you please share your experience? Leaving feedback is as easy as answering any of these questions:

- What did you like about the book?
- What is your most important takeaway or insight?
- What have you done differently--or what will you do differently because of what you have read?
- To whom would you recommend this book?

Of course, I'm looking for honest reviews. So if you have a minute to share your experience, good or bad, simply click here to leave your review: Amazon Review.

I look forward to hearing from you!

Sincerely,

COFFEE SHOP CONVERSATIONS

About The Author

Jed is passionate about helping people live happy, healthy, more connected lives by having better conversations. He is a husband, father of four girls, a psychology professor, therapist, and writer.

Jed graduated from Southern California Seminary with a Masters of Divinity and returned to complete a second master's degree in psychology. In his free time, Jed enjoys walking on the beach, reading, and spending time with his incredible family.

Continue the Conversation

    If you enjoyed this book, I would love it if you would leave a review on Amazon. As a new author, your feedback is a huge encouragement and helps books like this one get noticed. It only takes a minute, and every review is greatly appreciated. Oh, and please feel free to stay in touch too!

E-mail: jed@coffeeshopconversations.com

Twitter: @jjurchenko

Facebook: Coffee Shop Conversations

More Creative Conversations

This book and other creative conversation starters are available at www.Amazon.com.

This book is for everyone who longs to help their kids pause their electronics, grow their social skills, and develop lifelong relationships through highly engaging conversations! It will show you how to connect with your kids, and how to help your kids connect with others.

131 Conversations That Engage Kids

More Creative Conversations

The average family spends less than eight hours together each week. Be above average! Take your family from distant to bonded with these meaningful conversation starters.

Each chapter introduces a core family value, followed by ten conversation starters encouraging your family to cultivate this Christ-honoring value in your home. Build a multitude of happy memories with this book the entire family will enjoy!

131 Creative Conversations for Families

45400849R00096

Made in the USA
Lexington, KY
16 July 2019